From Your Friends at *The Mailbox*®

Math MIND BUILDERS

Grade 2

Welcome to *Math Mind Builders*! This must-have resource is sure to reinforce math skills while developing critical-thinking skills. Packed with curriculum-based problems and puzzles covering a variety of math topics, this resource provides students with a school year's worth of problem-solving opportunities.

Project Manager:
Njeri Jones Legrand

Editor:
Denine T. Carter

Writer:
William Fitzhugh

Art Coordinator:
Pam Crane

Artists:
Pam Crane, Greg D. Rieves

Cover Artists:
Nick Greenwood, Clevell Harris, Kimberly Richard
www.themailbox.com

ISBN #1-56234-420-X

Manufactured in the United States

10 9 8 7 6 5 4 3 2

INCLUDED IN THIS BOOK

Each activity page features five mind-building math problems plus a more difficult bonus builder problem to boost students' critical-thinking skills. Inside you will find an assortment of problems designed to reinforce the math topics and skills that you teach. Featured topics and skills include the following:

- computation
- numeration
- geometry
- time
- money
- fractions
- place value
- patterns & relationships
- measurement
- problem solving
- graphing, probability, & statistics

HOW TO USE THIS BOOK

Use the activity pages in this book in a variety of ways to supplement your math curriculum.

For independent practice, duplicate the activity pages for students to use as morning work, problems of the day, free-time activities, or daily homework practice.

For partner or small-group practice, duplicate a desired activity page and give each pair or group a copy. Have students discuss possible strategies for solving the problems.

For whole-group problem-solving practice, make transparencies of the activity pages.

For a learning center activity, duplicate, laminate, and cut apart the activity pages. Group the resulting cards by topic and place specific skill cards at a center. Or, for a mixed review, place a variety of skill cards at a center.

For assessing students' understanding of math concepts, make individual student copies and have each student explain in writing how to solve each problem.

Computation

Write a number sentence to show the total number of birds.

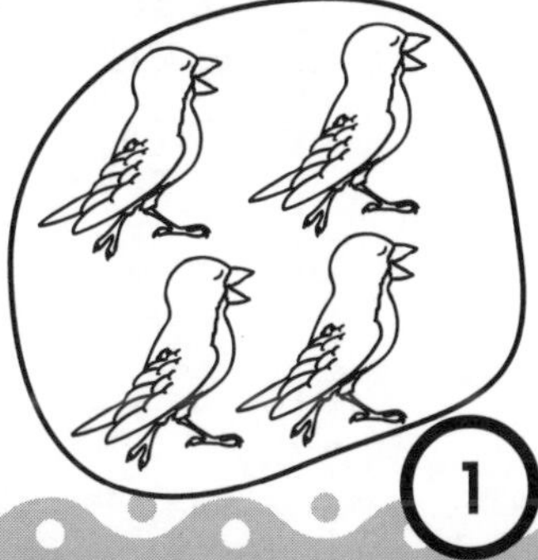

1

Place Value

I am a 2-digit number. I have a 9 in the tens place and a 5 in the ones place. What number am I?

2

Geometry

Draw and label a shape that has 3 sides. How many angles does it have?

3

Time

Lunch begins at 12:00 and ends in 1 hour. What time does lunch end?

4

Money

What 3 coins are in the bank?

5

Bonus Builder #1

Name the fraction for 1 slice of pizza.

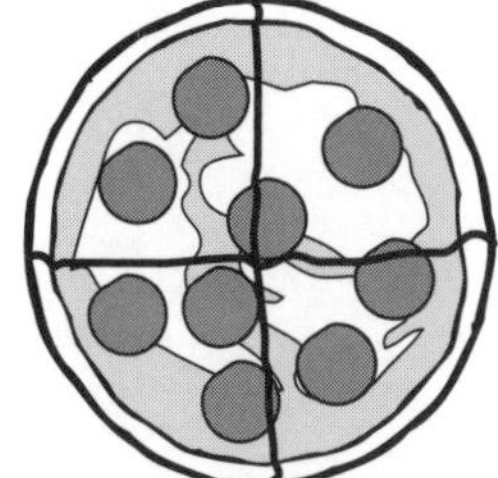

Fractions

Patterns & Relationships

Use the pattern to draw a necklace that has 12 beads.

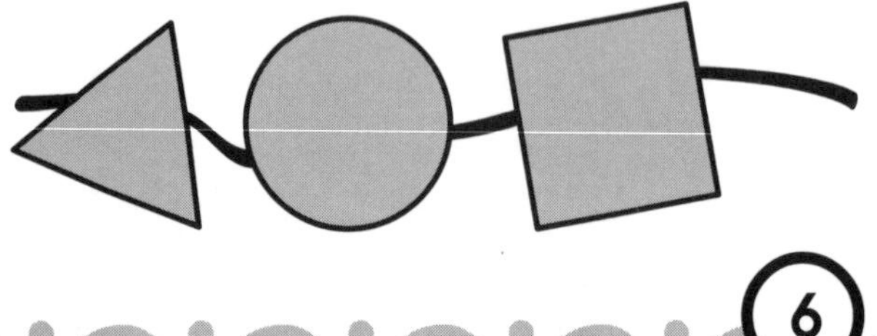

6

Measurement

Use your hand to measure across the top of your desk in palms and spans. Give each measure.

= palms
= spans

7

Problem Solving

Joe has 9 flowers. He puts the same number of flowers in each vase. How many flowers are in each vase?

8

Graphing, Probability, & Statistics

How many more students like apples than pears? How many students like pears and oranges all together?

Fruits	Number of Students
apple	🍎🍎🍎🍎🍎🍎🍎🍎
pear	🍐🍐🍐🍐
orange	🍊🍊🍊🍊🍊

9

Numeration

Write the numbers in order from least to greatest.

65 57 76 67

10

Bonus Builder #2

Write 3 more number sentences using the numerals 4, 5, and 9.

1. 9 – 4 = 5
2.
3.
4.

Computation

Geometry

Draw 2 different shapes that have 4 sides. Name each shape.

11

Computation

Write a number in each ○ to make each problem correct. Use a different set of numbers for each problem.

$\bigcirc + \bigcirc = 8$ $\bigcirc + \bigcirc = 8$ $\bigcirc + \bigcirc = 8$ $\bigcirc + \bigcirc = 8$ $\bigcirc + \bigcirc = 8$

12

Money

Amy bought a candy bar for 30¢. What 4 coins did she give the clerk?

13

Fractions

What fraction of the cake is missing?

14

Place Value

Write each number.

8 tens and 5 ones
4 tens and 9 ones
3 tens and 0 ones

15

Bonus Builder #3

Complete the pattern. Write the rule for the pattern.

100, 200, 300, ___, ___, ___, ___

Patterns & Relationships

MEASUREMENT

Would you use pounds, inches, or cups to measure the length of the pencil? Why?

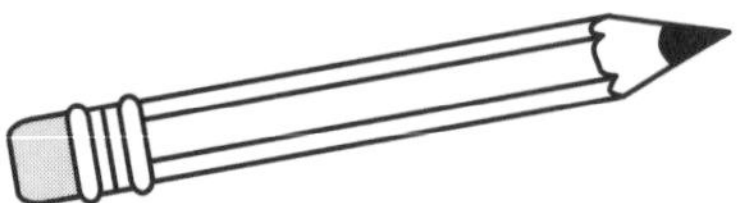

16

TIME

How many minutes long was the TV show?

Start

(1:30)

Finish

(2:00)

17

GRAPHING, PROBABILITY, & STATISTICS

Alice chooses a piece of candy without looking. Are her chances better for picking a square or round piece of candy? Explain your answer.

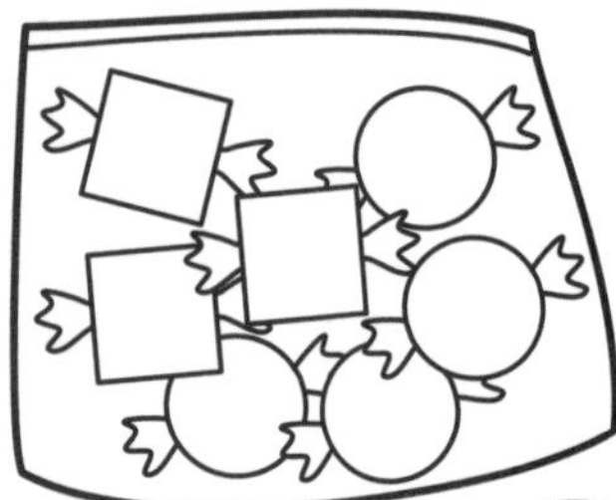

18

COMPUTATION

Which number sentence is incorrect? Explain your answer.

5 + 8 = 12
6 + 7 = 13
16 – 8 = 8

19

NUMERATION

List 5 odd numbers less than 20.

20

BONUS BUILDER #4

Which has more sides: 5 triangles or 4 squares?

GEOMETRY

TIME

What number will the minute hand point to when...

15 minutes have passed? ___

45 minutes have passed? ___

21

MONEY

List the coin names in order from least to greatest in value.

22

FRACTIONS

Which of these shapes is not divided into fourths? Explain your answer.

23

PLACE VALUE

Write each two-digit number. Use the key.

Key
△ = tens
○ = ones

○ △ ○ ○ △ ○ = ____

○ △ △ △ = ____

24

PATTERNS

Draw and describe the next monster in the pattern.

25

BONUS BUILDER #5

Use the inch ruler to estimate the length of your pencil.

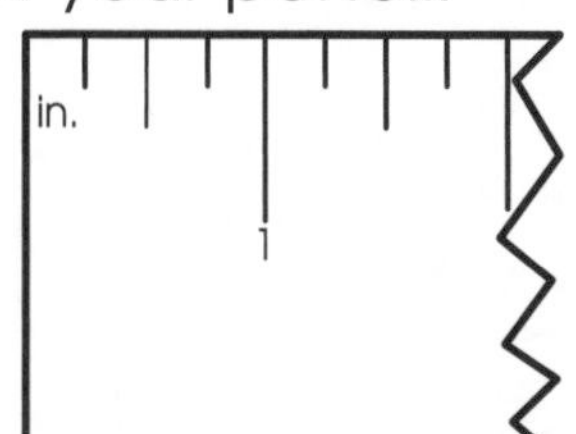

MEASUREMENT

Computation

Solve each problem.

$8 + \square = 17$

$\square - 5 = 12$

$15 - 9 = \square$

$6 + \square = 13$

26

Graphing, Probability, & Statistics

Use the bar graph. Which animals are equally liked? How many students like fish and birds all together?

Favorite Pets					
Pets	Number of Students				
cats	■	■	■		
fish	■	■	■	■	
birds	■	■	■		
	1	2	3	4	5

27

Problem Solving

Mrs. Jones lost 8 pencils. She found 3 of them. How many are still missing?

28

Numeration

I am an odd number that comes between 5 and 8. What number am I?

29

Geometry

Which of these is a closed shape? Draw a closed shape of your own.

A B  C D E

30

Bonus Builder #6

The minute hand is between the 3 and the 4. The hour hand is on the 8. List 4 possible times it could be.

Time

Money

How much are the coins? Draw a different set of coins that equals the same amount.

31

Fractions

Maria put $^{1}/_{2}$ of her fish in a bowl and $^{1}/_{2}$ in a pond. How many fish did she have all together?

32

Place Value

Put these in order from least to greatest.

2 tens 5 ones   18 ones   31 ones

33

Patterns & Relationships

Continue the pattern.

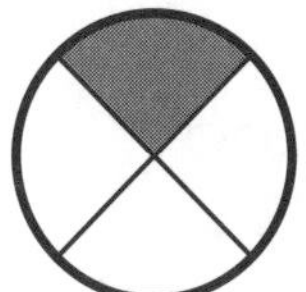

____

34

Measurement

A loaf of bread weighs about 1 pound. Which of these items also weighs about a pound?

eraser   basketball
feather   marble

35

Bonus Builder #7

Write three word problems using these cookies.

Problem Solving

Graphing, Probability, & Statistics

Read the chart. Write 3 sentences about how the students get to school.

Transportation	Number of Students
bus	~~IIII~~ II
car	~~IIII~~ ~~IIII~~ II
bike	III

36

Computation

Write 6 number sentences that have a sum of 10.

37

Numeration

Write the number for each word.

twenty-six
forty-five
fifty-nine
thirteen

38

Geometry

Name an object that has the same shape as each solid figure.

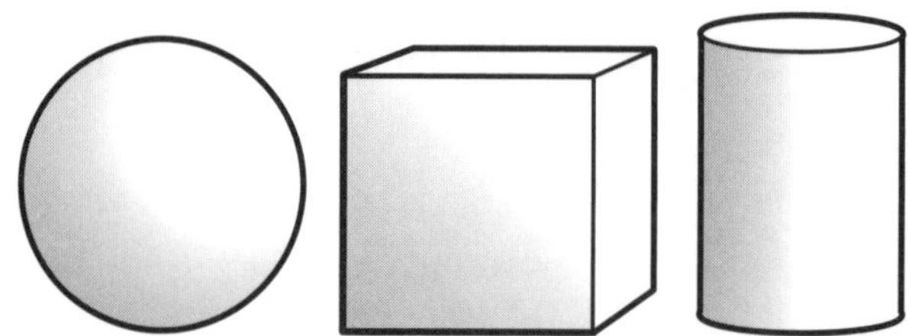

39

Time

Draw hands on the clock to show how the clock looks at noon and midnight.

40

Bonus Builder #8

Draw 6 coins that equal 27¢.

Money

NUMERATION

List all of the even numbers between 0 and 10.

41

PLACE VALUE

Write the numeral for each set of blocks.

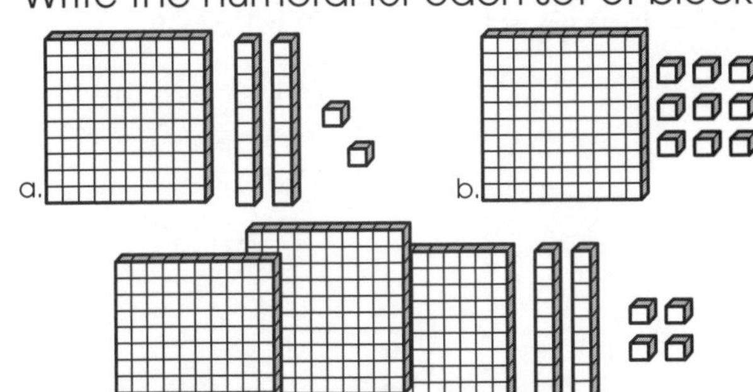

42

PATTERNS & RELATIONSHIPS

Complete the pattern. Write the rule.

10, 15, 20, ___, 30, 35, ___, ___

43

MEASUREMENT

Temperatures are shown for fall, winter, and summer. Label each thermometer with the correct season.

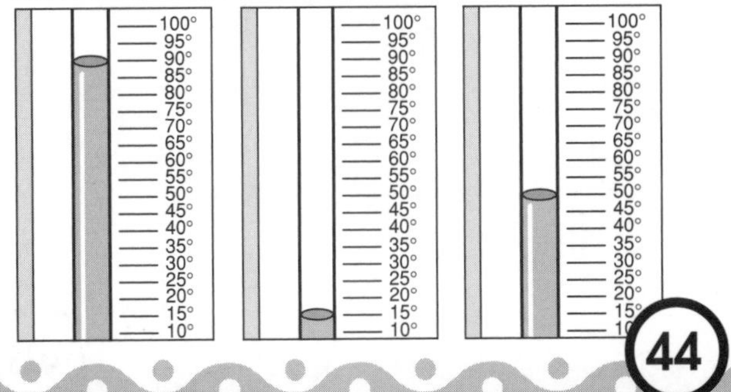

44

PROBLEM SOLVING

Evan is older than Alex, but younger than Jane. Their ages are 5, 10, and 12. How old is each person?

45

BONUS BUILDER #9

Label each fraction. Write < or > in each ○.

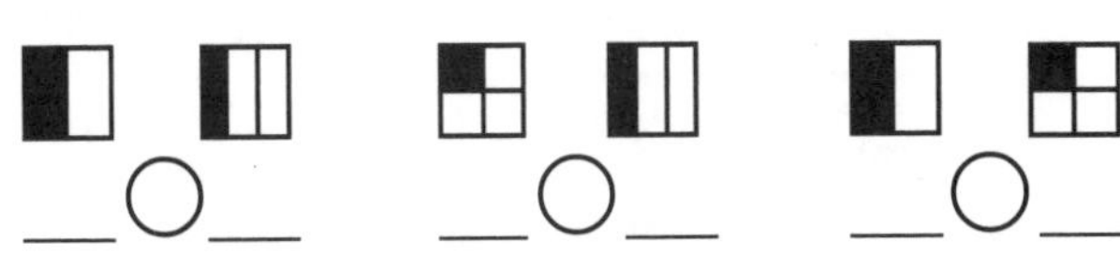

___ ○ ___ ___ ○ ___ ___ ○ ___

FRACTIONS

Computation

What is the sum of 8 and 26?

46

Numeration

Write <, >, or = in each □.

eighty □ 79
forty-three □ 34
nineteen □ 19

47

Geometry

A polygon is a closed, flat shape with 3 or more straight sides. Which is not a polygon?

○ △ □ ⏢

48

Time

It is half past 5. What is another way to say this time?

49

Money

Complete the chart.

___ pennies	$1.00
20 nickels	_____
___ dimes	$1.00
___ quarters	$1.00

50

Bonus Builder #10

How many students like vanilla more than chocolate?

How many students like vanilla more than strawberry?

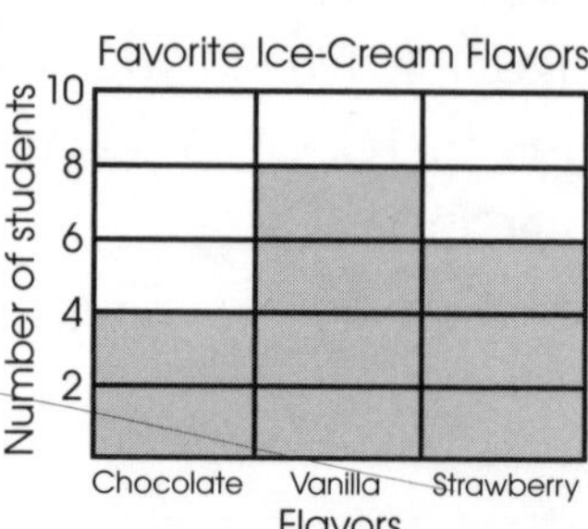

Graphing, Probability, & Statistics

Numeration

Write the numbers that come before and after each number.

___, ___, 45, ___, ___

___, ___, 76, ___, ___

51

Patterns & Relationships

Complete the pattern.

A1, B2, C3, ___, ___, F6, ___

52

Measurement

Match each object with the unit of measurement you would use. Draw a line to connect the dots.

distance to school	•	• gallons
amount of milk	•	• pounds
weight of an apple	•	• miles
perimeter of your room	•	• feet

53

Problem Solving

Count the money below. If you spent 28¢, what would your change be?

54

Graphing, Probability, & Statistics

On which color would you most likely land? Why?

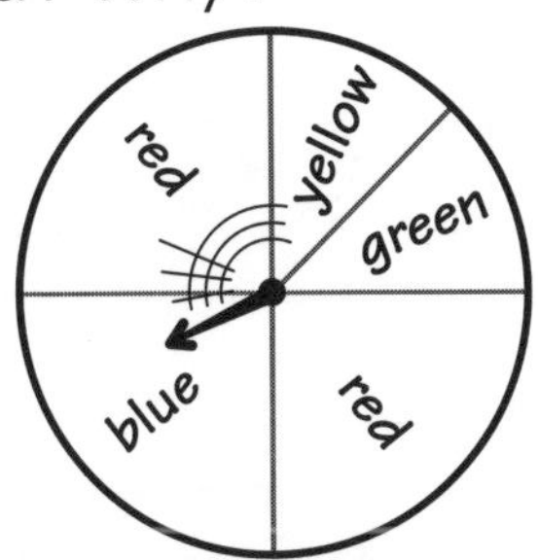

55

Bonus Builder #11

Write 2 different ways to complete the number sentence.

□ + □ + □ + □ + □ = 50

Computation

NUMERATION

Cross out the first car.
Circle the third car.
Underline the fifth car.

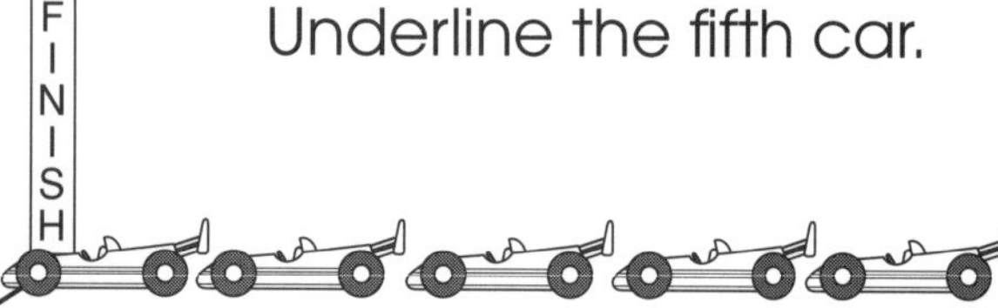

56

GEOMETRY

Draw 2 lines of symmetry on each figure.

57

MONEY

If you pay for the candy with 2 quarters, how much change will you get back? Draw and label your change.

58

FRACTIONS

Three children slice a pie into 3 equal slices. What fraction of the pie does each child get?

59

PLACE VALUE

Jeff has 3 bags of jelly beans plus 5 extra. How many jelly beans does he have all together?

60

BONUS BUILDER #12

What will be the tenth shape in the pattern?

PATTERNS & RELATIONSHIPS

TIME

Write each unit of time in order from shortest to longest in length.

week hour day minute year

PROBLEM SOLVING

Fred has 27 toys. Mike has 29 toys. Kate has more toys than Fred, but less toys than Mike. How many toys does Kate have?

62

GEOMETRY

Which shape is the same as ?

A 

B 

C 

D 

COMPUTATION

Sam won 5 games last week. He won 3 games this week. All together, did he win more or less than 7 games?

64

NUMERATION

I am more than 25 and less than 35. You say me when you skip-count by 5. What number am I?

65

BONUS BUILDER #13

Each day the class sold tickets for the school play. They sold 40 tickets in all. Complete the graph to show how many tickets were sold on Friday.

Days	Number of Tickets Sold
Monday	
Tuesday	
Wednesday	
Thursday	
Friday	
	= 2 tickets

GRAPHING, PROBABILITY, & STATISTICS

 • *Mind Builders* • *Math* • TEC1601 • Key p. 46

TIME

A train leaves the station at 9:00 and arrives in the next town at 9:45. How long was the trip?

66

FRACTIONS

What fraction of the doughnuts have sprinkles?

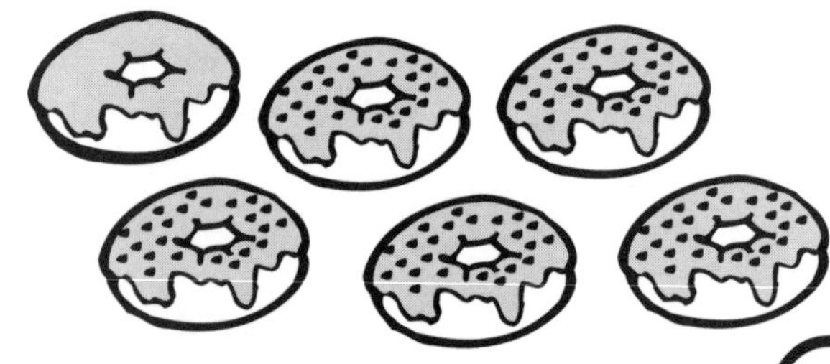

67

PLACE VALUE

Write the number.

4 hundreds 3 tens 9 ones

68

PATTERNS & RELATIONSHIPS

Draw the fifth figure in the pattern.

69

MEASUREMENT

Number the objects 1–4 from lightest to heaviest.

70

BONUS BUILDER #14

I am a two-digit number between 25 and 35. The sum of my digits is 4. What number am I?

COMPUTATION

Computation

Tom buys a lollipop for 15¢. His change is 10¢. Which coin did he give the clerk—a penny, a nickel, a dime, or a quarter?

71

Numeration

The piece below was cut from a hundreds board. Fill in the missing numbers.

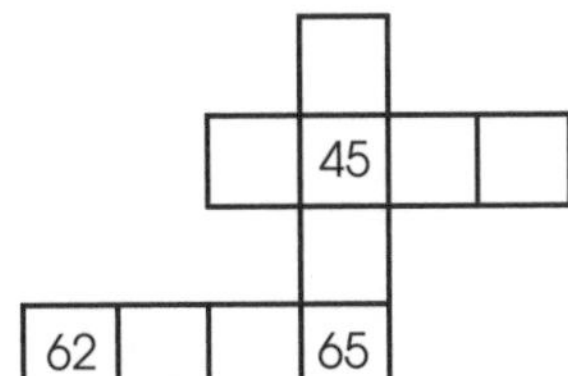

72

Geometry

How many sides and angles are in each polygon?

73

Time

Name the third, sixth, and tenth months of the year.

74

Fractions

How full is each jar? Color each jar to match the fraction.

$^1/_2$ $^1/_3$ $^1/_4$

75

Bonus Builder #15

Complete the pattern. Explain the rule.

1, 2, 4, 7, ___, 16, ___

Patterns & Relationships

Place Value

Add 10 to each number.

35, 76, 12, 93

76

Patterns & Relationships

How many ● should be added to Side B to balance the scale?

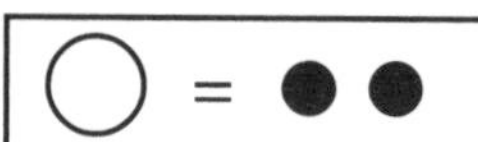

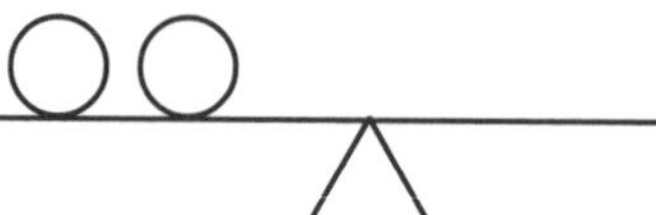

Side A Side B

77

Measurement

Sort the measurements into 2 groups. Label each group.

pound	inch	ton
gram	feet	centimeter

78

Numeration

Bob collected 7 stickers. How many more stickers does he need for a dozen?

79

Computation

How many golf balls can you buy with $1.00?

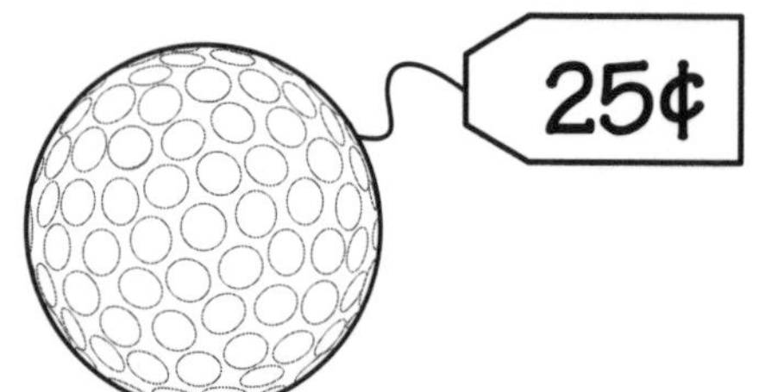

80

Bonus Builder #16

Jay may choose 1 item to eat and 1 item to drink for breakfast. What are the 4 different breakfasts he can choose?

bagel muffin milk juice

Problem Solving

Money

Look at the key. What is the total value of your name?

81

Geometry

If the points were connected, what shape would they make? Draw and label the shape.

82

Time

Pam arrives at the dentist at 12:45 and waits for 15 minutes. What time does she see the dentist?

83

Fractions

Draw a pattern in each box to complete the key.

Key

☐ = 5/8

☐ = 3/8

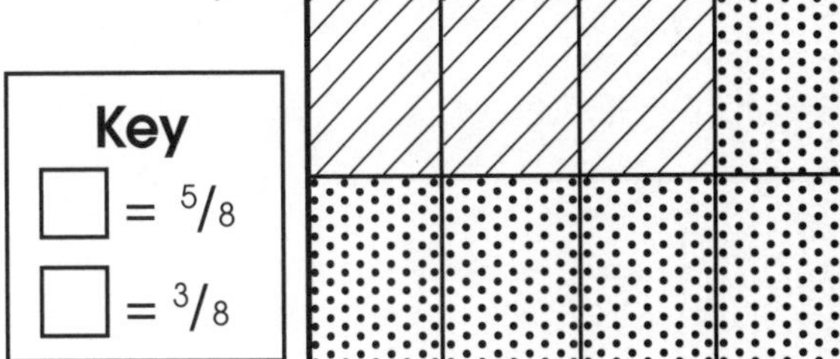

84

Place Value

Complete the chart.

10 less	number	10 more
	623	
		486
148		
	637	

85

Bonus Builder #17

There are 7 days in 1 week. How many days are in 2 weeks?

Problem Solving

Graphing, Probability, & Statistics

The students voted for their favorite sports. Color the graph to show the results.

sport	tally
basketball	卌 III
soccer	卌 卌
football	卌 I

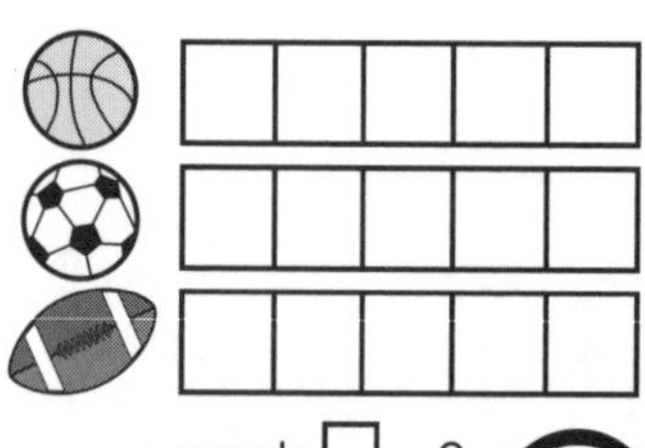

each ☐ = 2

86

Measurement

Draw and color 3 tools that people use for measuring.

87

Problem Solving

Sort the words into 2 groups.

addition
difference
minus
sum
subtraction
plus

88

Patterns & Relationships

Draw 2 figures in the middle section that belong in both sets.

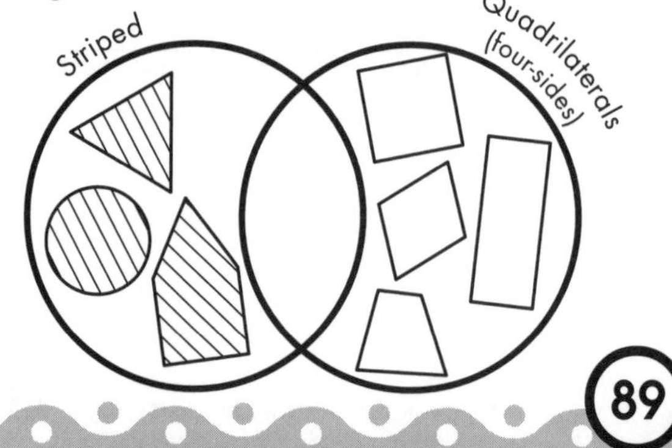

89

Computation

Each elephant has 10 peanuts. How many peanuts do they have all together?

90

Bonus Builder #18

For each number write the number that is 100 more.

517	826	490	377
319	204	759	637

Place Value

Geometry

Shapes A and D are *congruent.* Explain what you think the word congruent means. Draw 2 more congruent shapes.

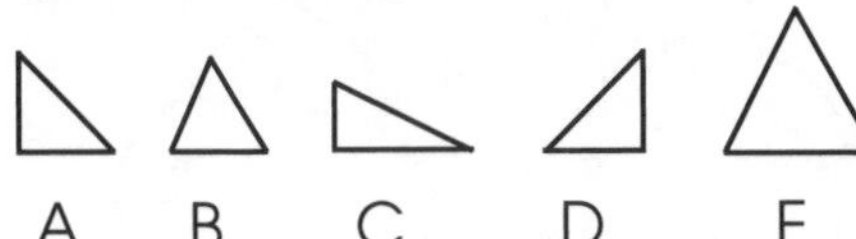

91

Time

A plane took off at 2:30 and landed 3 hours later. What time did the plane land?

92

Money

Bob and Sue have the same amount of money. What 2 coins does Sue have?

93

Fractions

Color 1/3 of the butterflies.

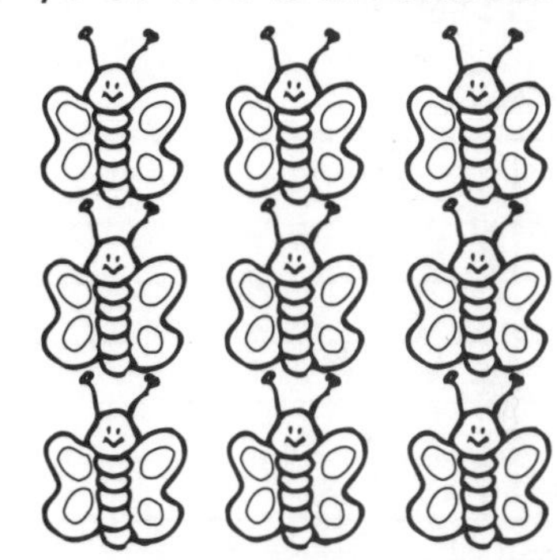

94

Patterns & Relationships

Draw the next shape in the pattern.

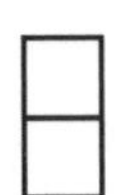

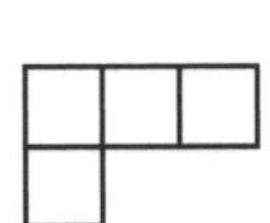

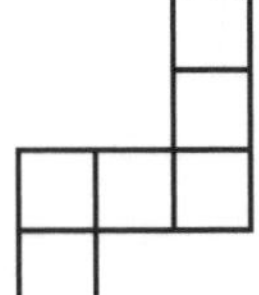

95

Bonus Builder #19

Write each number in expanded form. The first one is done for you.

527 = 500 + 20 + 7

652 = ___ + ___ + ___

436 = ___ + ___ + ___

Place Value

MEASUREMENT

Study the rectangle. What is the length of the missing side? What is the total length of the sides?

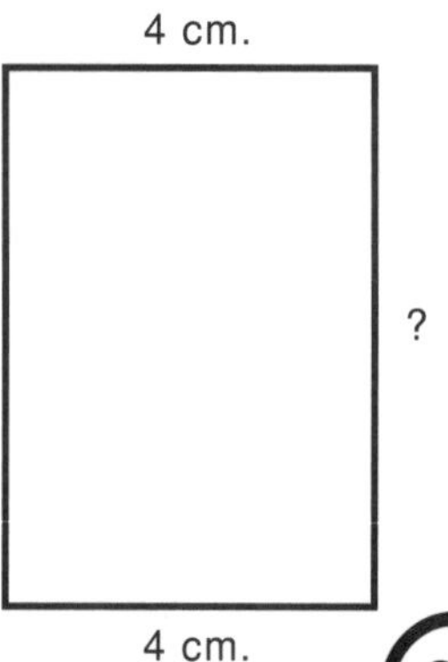

96

PROBLEM SOLVING

The rabbits shared 8 carrots equally. How many carrots did each rabbit have?

97

GRAPHING, PROBABILITY, & STATISTICS

Use the graph to answer the question about spring break.

How many more people went to the mountains than to the beach?

Spring Break Activities	Number of People
go camping	🯅 🯅 🯅
go to beach	🯅 🯅 🯅 🯅 🯅
stay home	🯅 🯅
visit relative	🯅 🯅 🯅 🯅
go to mountains	🯅 🯅 🯅 🯅 🯅 🯅
each 🯅 = 2 people	

98

GEOMETRY

Which 2 pieces could you use to form a square?

99

NUMERATION

Write the word name for each number.

15, 30, 100

100

BONUS BUILDER #20

Is the sum of 22 and 35 greater than or less than the sum of 13 and 42?

COMPUTATION

Fractions

Which fraction of the birds is in the nest?
Which fraction is not in the nest?

101

Money

Write < or > to compare the sets of coins.

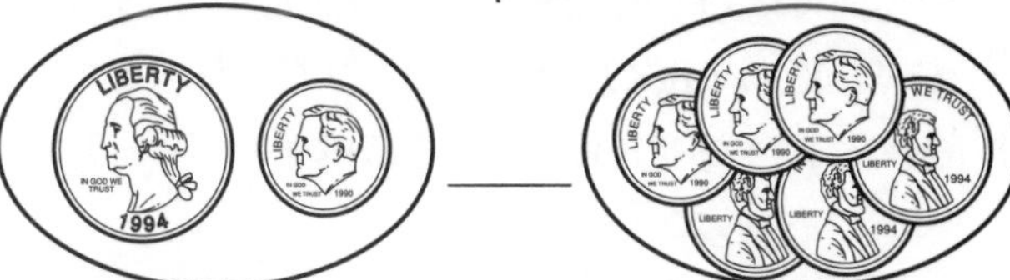

102

Time

What is the date for the second Monday in the month? The last Thursday? The fourth Wednesday?

JANUARY						
S	M	T	W	T	F	S
	1	2	3	4	5	6
7	8	9	10	11	12	13
14	15	16	17	18	19	20
21	22	23	24	25	26	27
28	29	30	31			

103

Place Value

Write the number in each ☐.

2 hundreds, 15 tens, and 2 ones = ☐

6 hundreds, 3 tens, and 25 ones = ☐

4 hundreds and 42 ones = ☐

1 hundred, 25 tens, and 7 ones = ☐

104

Patterns & Relationships

Complete the table.

clover	1	2	3	4	5	6	7	8	9	10
leaves	3		9				21			30

105

Bonus Builder #21

A peanut weighs about 3 grams. List 5 more items that may weigh about 3 grams.

Measurement

Problem Solving

Mark has 6 dogs. Larry has 4 cats. Sue has 4 dogs. Eli has 5 cats. Are there more dogs or cats?

106

Graphing, Probability, & Statistics

Tim has a bag with 2 oranges, 4 bananas, and 2 apples. Which fruits does he have an equal chance of picking from the bag? Explain your answer.

Computation

The children need 18 players to play a game. There are 15 children on the playground. How many more children do they need?

Numeration

List the numbers from least to greatest.

288, 384, 238, 586, 484

Geometry

What shape is the flat side of the cone?

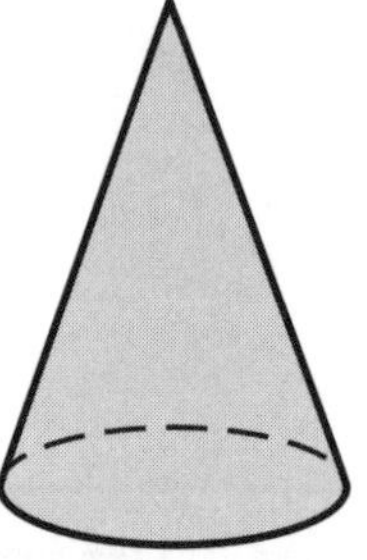

110

Bonus Builder #22

Is the sum of the Saturday dates greater than or less than the sum of the Tuesday dates?

FEBRUARY

S	M	T	W	T	F	S
				1	2	3
4	5	6	7	8	9	10
11	12	13	14	15	16	17
18	19	20	21	22	23	24
25	26	27	28			

Time

Money

Danny has 1 quarter and 2 dimes. How much more money does he need to buy the snow cone?

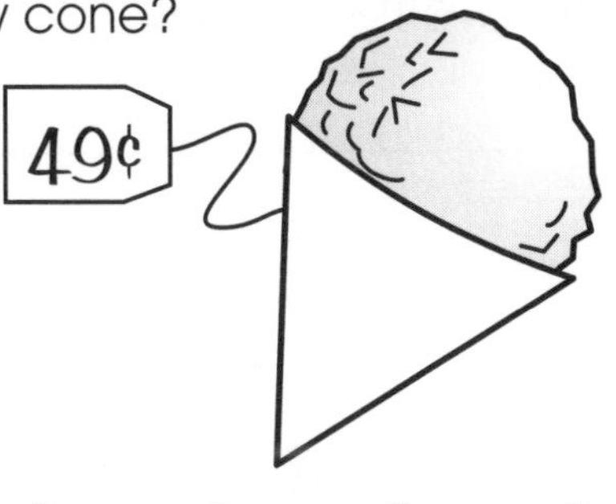

111

Fractions

Which fraction is largest: $^1/_2$ or $^1/_3$? Explain your answer.

112

Place Value

Start with the number 125. Add 2 ones, 5 tens, and 3 hundreds. What is the new number?

113

Patterns & Relationships

Draw the next 5 symbols in the pattern.

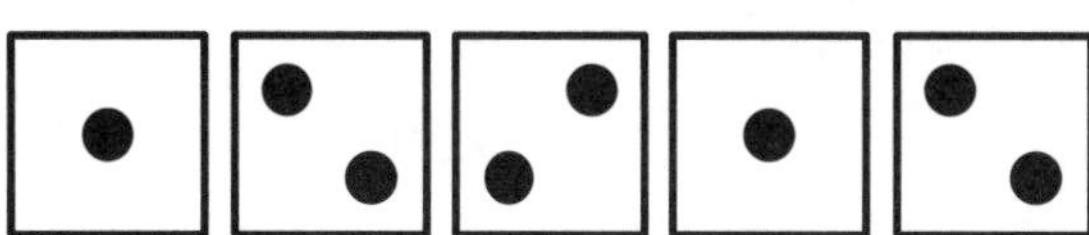

114

Measurement

The chalk weighs 4 grams. How much does the crayon weigh?

115

Bonus Builder #23

If 1 starfish has 5 arms, how many arms do 4 starfish have all together?

MONEY

What is the fewest amount of bills you could use to make $27? List the bills.

COMPUTATION

Which pair of numbers has a sum of 8 and a difference of 2?

5 and 7
2 and 8
2 and 6
3 and 5

NUMERATION

Compare the numbers. Write < or > in each ☐.

483 ☐ 438
832 ☐ 823
705 ☐ 750
4,070 ☐ 7,040

118

GEOMETRY

Mike has 2 figures. They have a total of 10 sides. Which 2 shapes does he have?

trapezoid pentagon

hexagon

TIME

Write the date that is one month and one day later than your birthdate.

120

BONUS BUILDER #24

Write 2 numbers in each section of the diagram.

Even Numbers

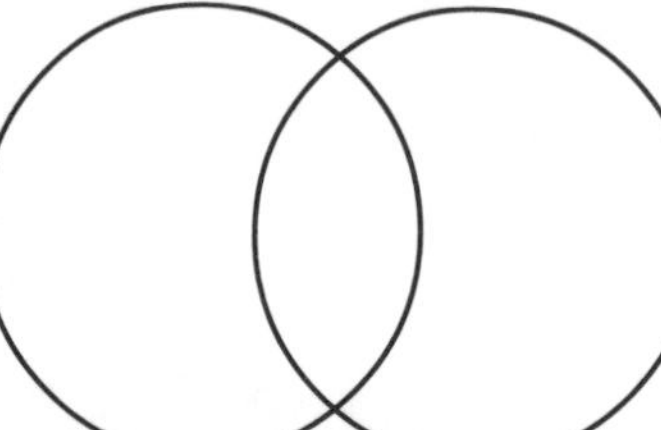

Numbers Greater Than 100

PATTERNS & RELATIONSHIPS

Fractions

Illustrate each fraction. List the fractions from least to greatest.

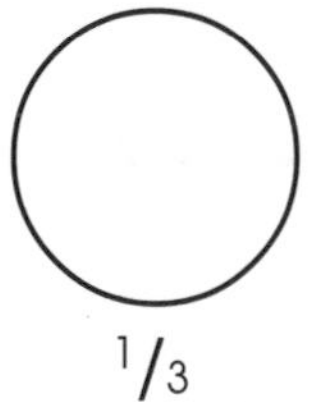

$^1/_3$

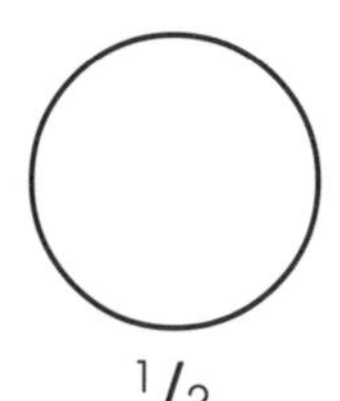

$^1/_2$

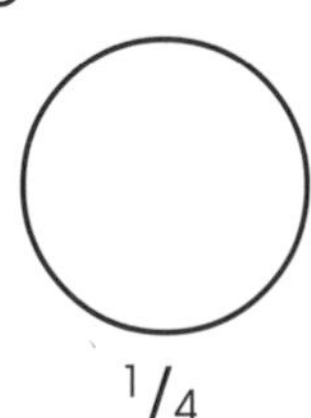

$^1/_4$

121

Place Value

Write the value of 1 in each number.

1,389 617 51 138

122

Patterns & Relationships

Fill in the missing numbers.

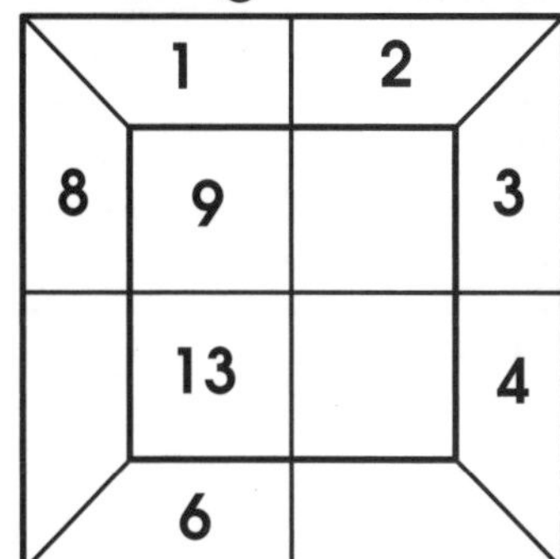

123

Geometry

How many triangles would it take to fill the trapezoid?

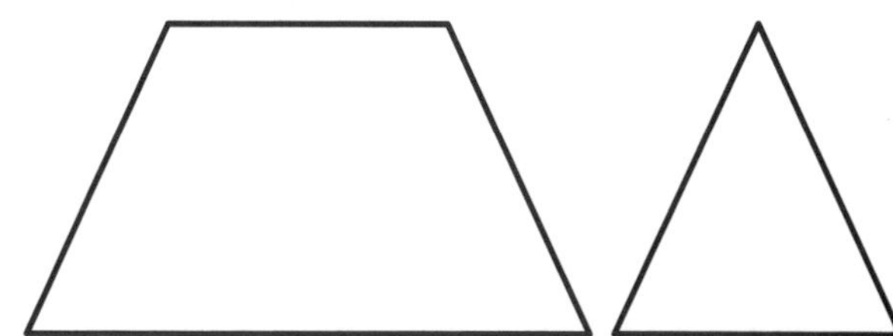

124

Problem Solving

Explain how you could solve the problem below.

Andy swims 10 laps a day. How many laps does he swim in 7 days?

125

Bonus Builder #25

Use the information to make a bar graph showing the students' favorite fruits.

- 4 students like bananas
- 10 students like oranges
- 8 students like apples
- 7 students like grapes

Graphing, Probability, & Statistics

COMPUTATION

Check each problem. Fix the problems that are incorrect.

$$\begin{array}{r} 554 \\ +\ 153 \\ \hline 707 \end{array} \quad \begin{array}{r} 172 \\ +\ 595 \\ \hline 777 \end{array} \quad \begin{array}{r} 348 \\ +\ 638 \\ \hline 986 \end{array} \quad \begin{array}{r} 385 \\ +\ 194 \\ \hline 589 \end{array}$$

126

NUMERATION

Label each point on the number line.

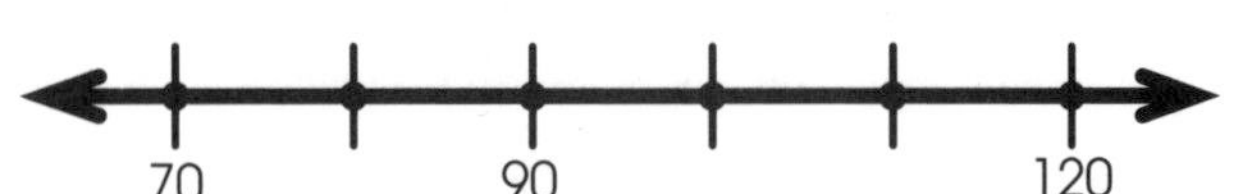

127

GEOMETRY

What is the total square centimeters shaded in the graph?

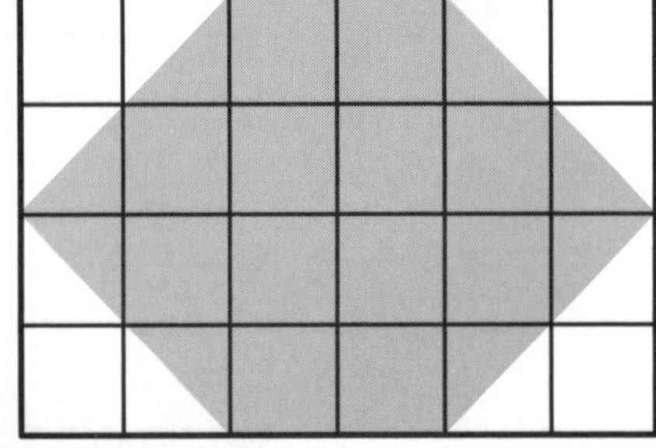

□ = 1 square cm.

128

TIME

Complete the chart.

___ minutes	1 hour
___ hours	1 day
___ days	1 week

129

MONEY

Jack has $1.30. How much more money does he need to buy the yo-yo?

130

BONUS BUILDER #26

Nancy uses 1/4 cup chocolate chips to make 12 cookies. How many cups would she use to make 24 cookies? 48 cookies?

FRACTIONS

Place Value

Write the number shown. Use the key.

Key

= ones

= tens

= hundreds

= thousands

131

Patterns & Relationships

Study the pattern. Use the same rule to make a pattern with circles and squares.

132

Measurement

Draw a thermometer that reads 50°F. Then draw a picture to show how you would dress if that were the temperature.

133

Problem Solving

Ms. Johnson has 11 girls and 17 boys in her class. How many pieces of candy would she have to bring to school to give each student 2 pieces?

134

Computation

Write the pair of numbers that has a sum of 50.

15, 16, 19, 26, 34

135

Bonus Builder #27

If you reached in the jar with your eyes closed and pulled out 6 marbles, how many of the shaded marbles do you think you would get? Explain your answer.

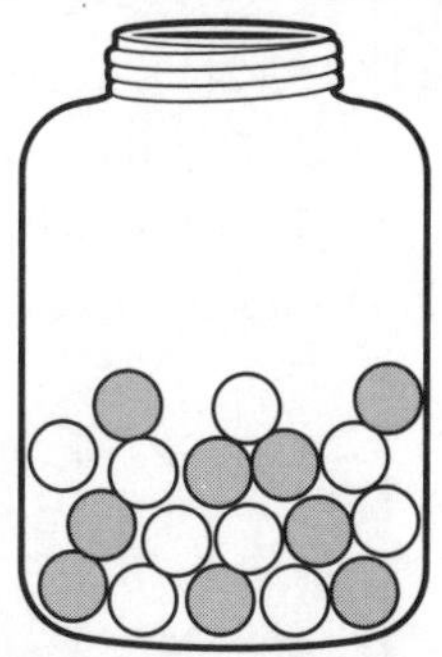

Graphing, Probability, & Statistics

Numeration

Kenya has 2 pairs of shoes. Her brother has 3 pairs of shoes. How many shoes do they have all together?

136

Geometry

Which figure is not a polygon? Explain your answer.

A B C D

137

Time

Jessica left for New York at 6:15 A.M. and arrived at 8:15 A.M. How long was her trip?

138

Money

Which 6 coins equal 1 dollar?

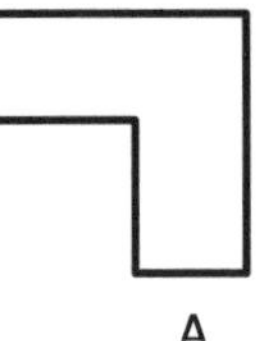

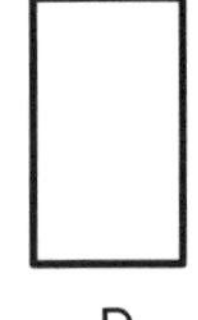

139

Fractions

Study each circle. If 3/4 is shaded, draw a box around the circle. If more than 3/4 is shaded, underline the circle. If less than 3/4 is shaded, draw an *X* over the circle.

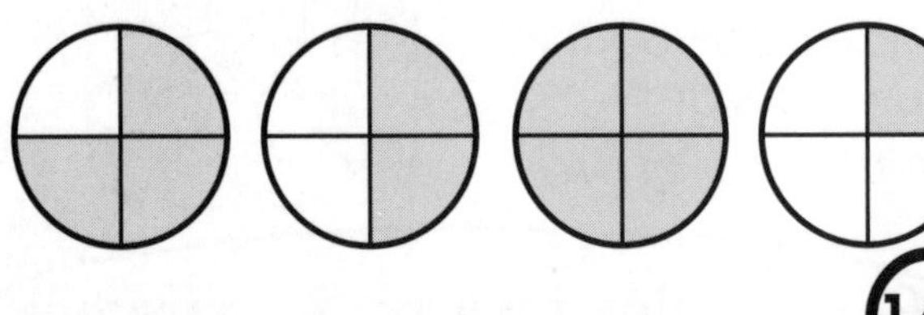

140

Bonus Builder #28

Write two number sentences to solve the problem.

Mark buys 25 gumballs. He gives 10 to Maya. Then he chews 7 gumballs himself. How many gumballs does he have left?

Computation

Problem Solving

Ed plants 5 tomato plants on each side of his square garden. How many tomato plants are there in all?

141

Numeration

Which numbers are odd and greater than 12?

9, 13, 16, 14, 5, 11, 21

142

Geometry

List the animals on the grid. Write the number pair for each animal.

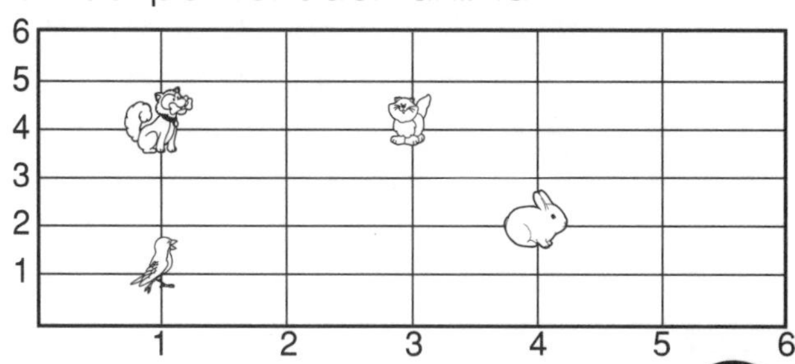

143

Time

Anthony left for his dentist appointment at 3:30 P.M. and got there half an hour later. Was he on time for his 3:45 P.M. appointment? Explain your answer.

144

Graphing, Probability, & Statistics

Draw a spinner using the shapes below so that the spinner is most likely to land on the square.

 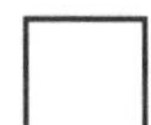  

145

Bonus Builder #29

I am a three-digit number less than 200. The digit in the tens place is 2 times more than the digit in the ones place. The digit in the ones place is 2. What number am I?

Place Value

Computation

Write a pair of single-digit numbers that has a sum of 14 and a difference of 4.

Place Value

Write each number in expanded form.

869 = ____________________

2,418 = ____________________

305 = ____________________

Geometry

How could you sort the figures into 2 groups? 3 groups?

triangle	cube	circle
sphere	square	pyramid

148

Money

Seeds cost 20¢ per pack. How many packs can you buy for $1.00?

149

Fractions

If 3 students share the cheese pizza equally and 4 students share the pepperoni pizza equally, which pizza slices will be bigger—cheese or pepperoni? Explain your answer.

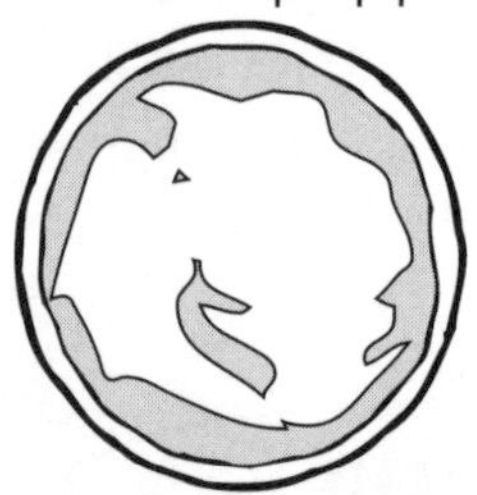

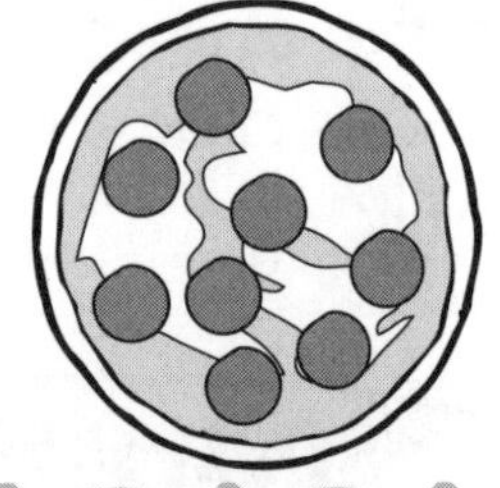

150

Bonus Builder #30

How many possible ways could Dan, Jan, and Stan line up? List the possible ways.

Problem Solving

Numeration

Write the first, fourth, sixth, and seventh letters of the word *numeration.* What word did you spell?

Time

Write the days and the dates that are one day before and 1 day after Friday, October 12.

152

Geometry

Write your name. Circle any symmetrical letters in your name.

153

Measurement

Write the units of measurement from smallest to largest.

pint   cup   gallon   quart

Money

What 7 coins could you use to make 77¢?

155

Bonus Builder #31

Solve the problem. What information was not needed to solve the problem?

Jan picked 15 apples. Later she picked 2 apples and 10 pears. How many apples did she pick in all?

Problem Solving

Numeration

I am the second odd number between 334 and 340. What number am I?

156

Patterns & Relationships

Find and explain the mistake in this pattern.

0, 3, 6, 9, 11, 15

157

Place Value

Which number does not belong? Explain your answer.

281 285 238 287 286

158

Problem Solving

Mary bought a dozen white eggs and a half-dozen brown eggs. How many eggs did she buy all together?

159

Graphing, Probability, & Statistics

How many flowers are in Joy's garden? How many flowers are there all together?

Flowers in Gardens	
Roy	✿✿✿
Pete	✿✿
Joy	✿✿✿✿
✿ = 5 flowers	

160

Bonus Builder #32

You buy a can of soda for 45¢ and a cookie for 30¢. If you pay with $1.00, how much is your change?

Money

Numeration

Write a number for each word. List the numbers from least to greatest.

ninety-one forty-seven
one hundred twenty-three

161

Geometry

Count the number of lines used to draw the 3 triangles. How many lines would it take to draw 5 triangles?

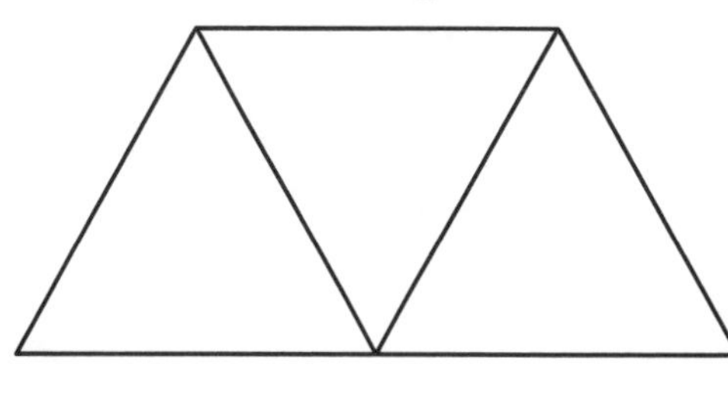

162

Money

Matthew has 1 dollar, 7 quarters, and 2 pennies. Lori has 2 dollars, 7 dimes, and 3 pennies. Who has the most money?

163

Fractions

Half of the pencils are red. One-fourth of the pencils are blue. How many of the pencils are yellow?

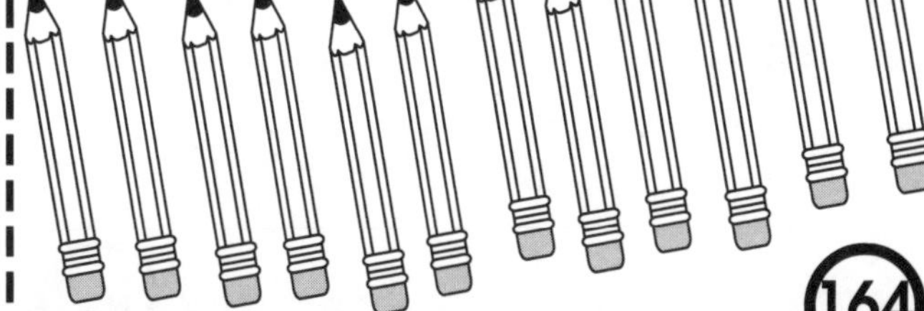

164

Place Value

Choose 4 different numerals from 1 to 9. Use the numerals to make as many four-digit numbers as you can.

165

Bonus Builder #33

Is the tree taller or shorter than 12 feet? Explain your answer.

Measurement

Computation

Solve each problem. Circle the sums greater than 100.

34 + 66 =

43 + 58 =

56 + 44 =

62 + 38 =

55 + 50 =

166

Measurement

Ms. Carter needs 14 inches of ribbon. Will 1 foot of ribbon be enough? Explain your answer.

167

Money

You pay for an ice-cream cone that costs 65¢ and get 10¢ back in change. What 3 coins did you have before you bought the ice-cream cone?

168

Graphing, Probability, & Statistics

Make a pictograph to show the fast-food items ordered. Use the ○ symbol on your pictograph to equal 2 food items.

hamburger	8
cheeseburger	10
french fries	7
onion rings	3
chicken sandwich	9

169

Time

The horse show started at 9:15 A.M. and ended at 12:15 P.M. How long was the show?

170

Bonus Builder #34

John pressed 9 on the calculator. Then he pressed 5 more keys and the number 27 came up on the calculator. Which 5 keys could he have pressed?

Problem Solving

GEOMETRY

List 3 ways squares and rectangles are alike.

171

PROBLEM SOLVING

Adam has 3 apples. Brandon has twice as many oranges. How many pieces of fruit does Brandon have? How many do they have all together?

172

FRACTIONS

What fraction of a dollar is 50¢?

173

MONEY

Jason has $1.00 to spend. Which 2 items can he buy?

174

COMPUTATION

How could you find the total number of frogs without counting each one?

175

BONUS BUILDER #35

The chart shows the times that Lauren's school bus arrived at school each day. What time will her bus most likely arrive on day 6? Explain your answer.

Bus Times	
Day 1	7:15
Day 2	7:15
Day 3	7:23
Day 4	7:15
Day 5	7:14

GRAPHING, PROBABILITY, & STATISTICS

MONEY

Austin pays for the balloon with 2 quarters. Draw his change.

176

PROBLEM SOLVING

If 4 children share the lollipops equally, how many lollipops will each child get?

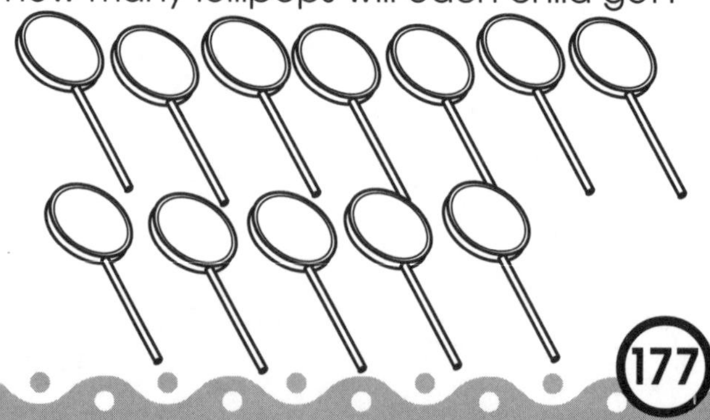

177

TIME

Taylor's preschool begins at 12:30 P.M. and ends at 3:30 P.M. How long is her school day?

178

COMPUTATION

Use the key to solve each problem.

Key

▲ = 25 ❍ = 30 ❑ = 45

A. ▲ + ❍ = ______
B. ❍ + ❍ = ______
C. ❑ + ▲ + ❍ = ______
D. ❑ – ▲ = ______

179

PLACE VALUE

Write the value of the 7 in each number.

786 4,067 876 7,302

180

BONUS BUILDER #36

Write a number sentence to show…

- the cost of 2 Rock Racer games
- the total cost of a Starship Zone game and a Zapp game

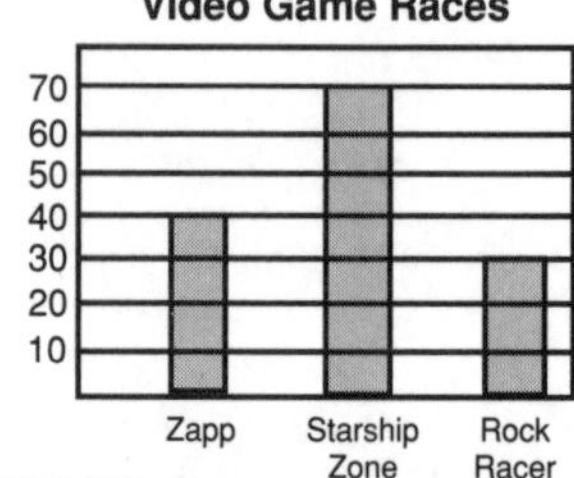

GRAPHING, PROBABILITY, & STATISTICS

Problem Solving

The bike rack is filled. Pam's bike is in the middle of the rack. There are 4 bikes to the right of Pam's bike. How many bikes does the rack hold?

181

Money

Who has more money? How much more?

Katie	
Danielle	

182

Place Value

I am a three-digit number that comes before 163. My ones digit is 8. The sum of my digits is 14. What number am I?

183

Patterns & Relationships

Complete the chart.

dozens	1	2		4	5
bagels	12	24	36		

184

Computation

How much would 7 stamps cost?

185

Bonus Builder #37

Phillip took 1/3 of his brother's marbles. How many marbles did he take? How many marbles does his brother have left?

Fractions

PROBLEM SOLVING

Each box holds 5 books. Fred has 20 books. Does he have enough boxes to hold all of his books?

Explain your answer.

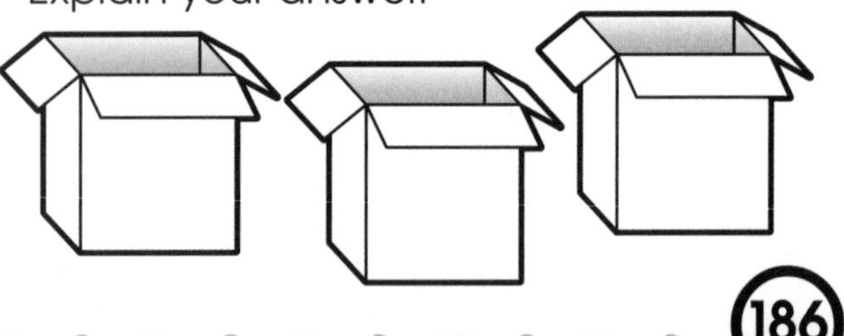

186

PATTERNS & RELATIONSHIPS

If the pattern repeats 3 times, how many stars will there be?

187

NUMERATION

Write the number that comes before and after each number.

___ 629 ___

___ 889 ___

___ 299 ___

188

GEOMETRY

What is the length of the missing side?

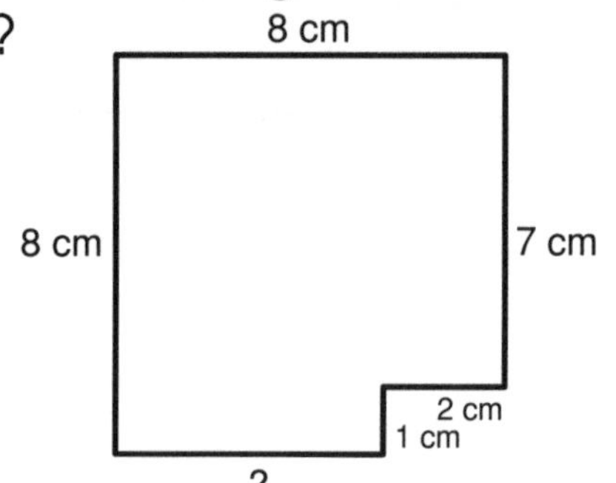

189

PLACE VALUE

What is the largest three-digit number you can make with 3 in the tens place? What is the smallest three-digit number you can make with 9 in the hundreds place?

190

BONUS BUILDER #38

You have $100 to spend. Name 2 items that you could buy. What would your change be?

MONEY

Computation

Jenny tossed 4 beanbags that landed on 4 different numbers. The numbers have a sum of 14. On which 4 numbers did Jenny's bags land?

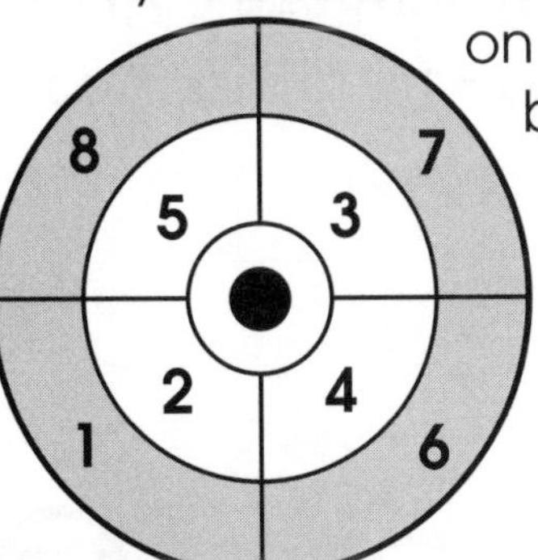

Fractions

Joey ate $5/8$ of the candy bar. How many pieces did he eat? How many were left?

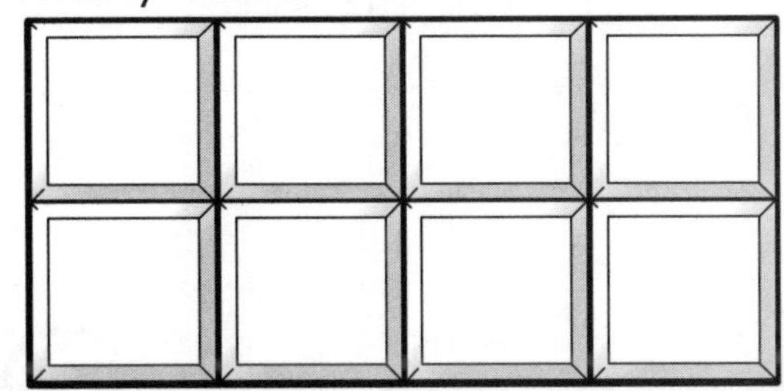

192

Measurement

Draw a line from each unit of measurement to its matching tool.

inches	scale
pint	ruler
feet	measuring cup
pounds	yardstick

193

Graphing, Probability, & Statistics

Complete the graph to show that the oak tree is 30 feet shorter than the pine tree and the maple tree is 50 feet taller than the dogwood tree.

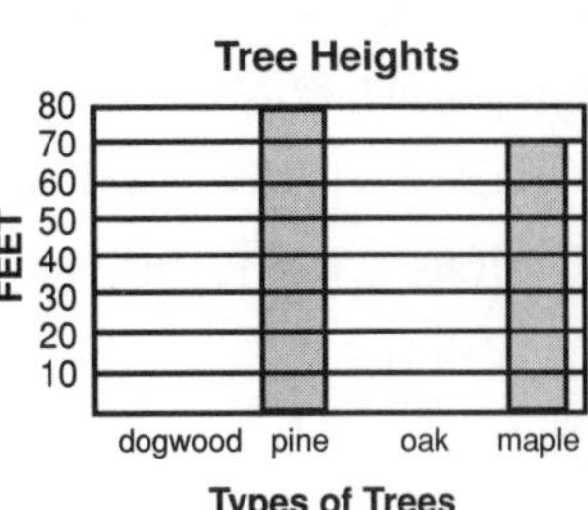

194

Place Value

Write each number in expanded form.

4,375 = ____ + ____ + ____ + ____

2,081 = ____ + ____ + ____ + ____

6,412 = ____ + ____ + ____ + ____

195

Bonus Builder #39

Tony has 5 coins that total 46¢. If 2 of his coins are the same, what 5 coins does Tony have?

Money

Patterns & Relationships

Complete the pattern.

_____; 100; 1,000; 10,000; _______

196

Numeration

List all of the even numbers that are greater than 526 but less than 538.

197

Problem Solving

Mike, Sara, and Joe each have a favorite color—red, yellow, or blue. Sara does not like red. Mike likes blue best. List each child's favorite color.

198

Time

Look at the schedule. What are the students doing at 10:45 A.M.? How much longer until the next activity?

Class Schedule	
Time	**Activity**
9:00–10:00	Math
10:00–11:00	Reading
11:00–11:30	Lunch
11:30–12:30	Science

199

Geometry

How many squares are in the figure?

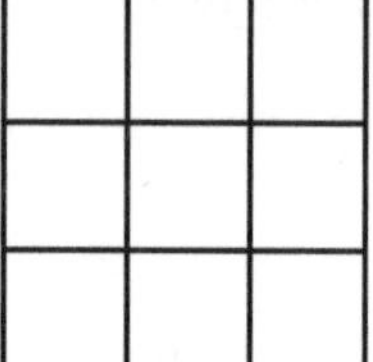

200

Bonus Builder #40

Jimmy, Timmy, and Kimmy each bought a gift for 3 friends. How many gifts were bought all together?

Problem Solving

Computation

Steve rode his bike for 24 miles. How many more miles must he ride to get to Town B?

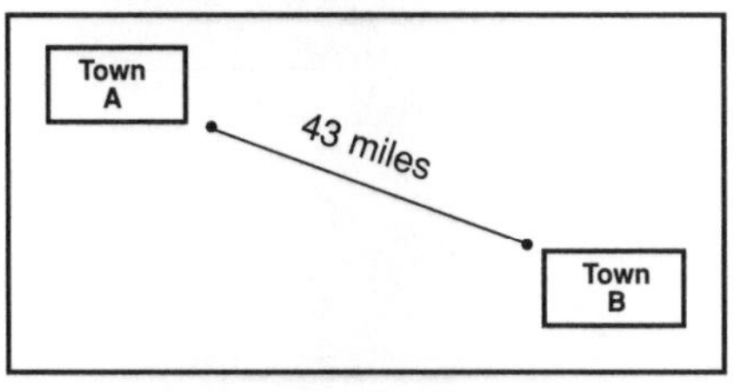

201

Fractions

There are 4 apple slices, 2 orange slices, and 3 grapes in the fruit bowl. What fraction of the fruit do the grapes make up?

202

Patterns & Relationships

Complete the pattern.

     ______

______ ______

Graphing, Probability, & Statistics

There are 25 students in the class. 18 students voted. How many did not vote?

Geometry

Which 2 figures can be put together to make a square?

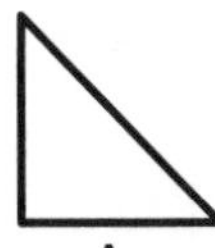
A.

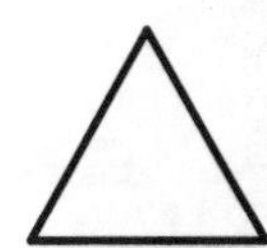
B.

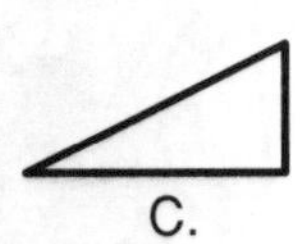
C.

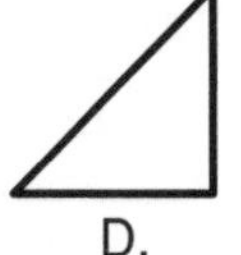
D.

205

Bonus Builder #41

Complete the chart.

Number	H	T	O	Sum of digits
		2	3	9
	5	0		7
233	2	3	3	

Place Value

Fractions

Half the letters in the boy's name are vowels. Is his name Rob, John, Noah, or Rick?

206

Time

Judy was born in 1996. Was her older brother born in 1999, 2000, 1994, or 1997?

207

Geometry

Draw a triangle. Then draw what it would look like if it were folded in half.

208

Computation

Freda sold 324 books on Friday and 148 books on Saturday. How many books did she sell all together?

Graphing, Probability, & Statistics

Mike, Anna, and Joe were playing a game. They used this spinner to decide who would go first. Is the spinner fair? Why or why not?

210

Bonus Builder #42

Donna filled her pitcher with milk, then poured the milk into 2 jars. In which jars did she pour the milk?

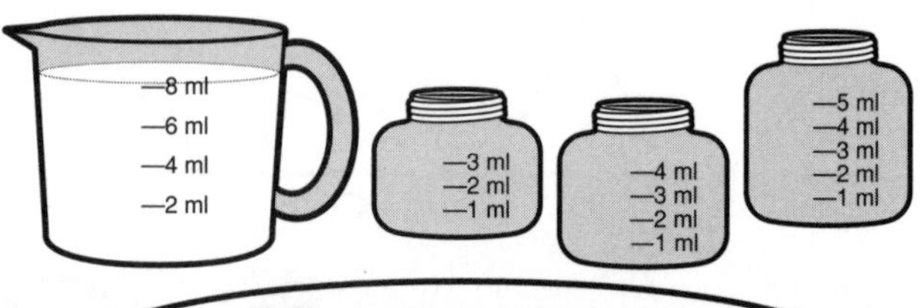

Measurement

Answer Keys

Page 3

1. 3 + 4 = 7
2. 95
3. Students should have drawn and labeled a triangle; 3 angles
4. 1:00 P.M.
5. dime, nickel, penny

Bonus Builder #1: $1/4$

Page 4

6. 
7. Answers will vary.
8. 3 flowers
9. 4 students; 9 students
10. 57, 65, 67, 76

Bonus Builder #2: Order of answers may vary.

1. 9 – 4 = 5
2. 9 – 5 = 4
3. 5 + 4 = 9
4. 4 + 5 = 9

Page 5

11. Students should have drawn and labeled 2 different shapes with 4 sides, such as a square and a rectangle.
12. Order of answers may vary.

$$\begin{array}{ccccc} ⓪ & ① & ② & ③ & ④ \\ +⑧ & +⑦ & +⑥ & +⑤ & +④ \\ \hline 8 & 8 & 8 & 8 & 8 \end{array}$$

13. 2 dimes and 2 nickels
14. $1/2$ or $3/6$
15. 85, 49, 30

Bonus Builder #3: 100, 200, 300, 400, 500, 600, 700; Pattern Rule: Add 100.

Page 6

16. inches; because inches measure length
17. a half hour (30 minutes)
18. Her chances are better for picking a round piece of candy because there is more round candy in the bag.
19. 5 + 8 = 12 is incorrect because 5 + 8 = 13.
20. Students should have listed 5 of the following numbers: 1, 3, 5, 7, 9, 11, 13, 15, 17, 19.

Bonus Builder #4: 4 squares

Page 7

21. 3; 9
22. penny, nickel, dime, quarter, half-dollar
23. ⊕; The four sections are not equal in size.
24. 24; 31
25. Students should have drawn or described a monster with 4 eyes and 4 antennae.

Bonus Builder #5: Answers will vary.

Page 8

26. 8 + $\boxed{9}$ = 17 $\boxed{17}$ – 5 = 12
    15 – 9 = $\boxed{6}$ 6 + $\boxed{7}$ = 13
27. cats and birds; 7 students
28. 5 pencils
29. 7
30. Figure B is the closed shape. Students should have drawn a closed shape.

Bonus Builder #6: 8:16, 8:17, 8:18, 8:19

Page 9

31. 40¢; Answers will vary.
32. 12 fish
33. 18 ones (18), 2 tens 5 ones (25), 31 ones (31)
34. 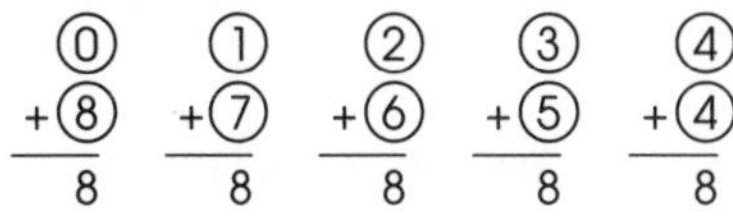
35. basketball

Bonus Builder #7: Answers will vary.

Page 10

36. Answers will vary.
37. 0 + 10 = 10, 1 + 9 = 10, 2 + 8 = 10, 3 + 7 = 10, 4 + 6 = 10, 5 + 5 = 10
38. 26, 45, 59, 13
39. Answers will vary.
40. 

Bonus Builder #8: Students should have drawn 1 dime, 3 nickels, and 2 pennies.

Page 11

41. 2, 4, 6, 8
42. a. 122
    b. 109
    c. 324
43. 10, 15, 20, 25, 30, 35, 40, 45; Pattern rule: Add 5.
44. 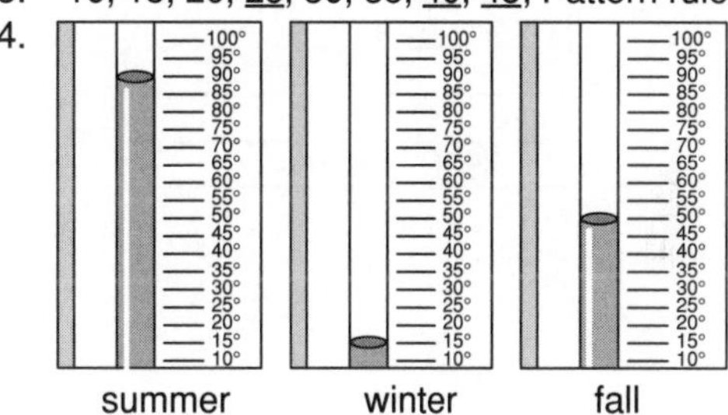

45. Evan—10, Alex—5, Jane—12

Bonus Builder #9: $1/2 > 1/3$, $1/4 < 1/3$, $1/2 > 1/4$

Page 12

46. 34
47. eighty $\boxed{>}$ 79
    forty-three $\boxed{>}$ 34
    nineteen $\boxed{=}$ 19
48. circle
49. five-thirty
50.

100 pennies	$1.00
20 nickels	$1.00
10 dimes	$1.00
4 quarters	$1.00

Bonus Builder #10: 4 students, 2 students

Page 13

51. 43, 44, 45, 46, 47
    74, 75, 76, 77, 78
52. A1, B2, C3, D4, E5, F6, G7
53. distance to school — miles
    amount of milk — gallons
    weight of an apple — pounds
    perimeter of your room — feet
54. 22¢
55. Red. This section is the largest.

Bonus Builder #11: Answers will vary. Possible solutions include the following:

$\boxed{10} + \boxed{10} + \boxed{10} + \boxed{10} + \boxed{10} = 50$

$\boxed{15} + \boxed{15} + \boxed{10} + \boxed{5} + \boxed{5} = 50$

Answer Keys

Page 14

56.

57. Possible answers:

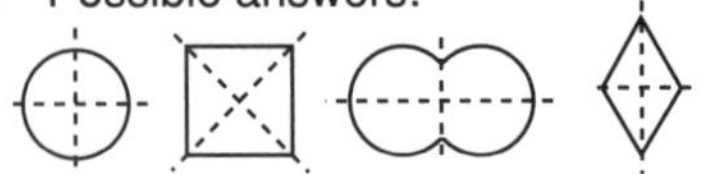

58. 10¢. Students' drawings will vary.
59. 1/3
60. 35

Bonus Builder #12: circle

Page 15

61. minute, hour, day, week, year
62. 28
63. C
64. more
65. 30

Bonus Builder #13:

Days	Number of Tickets Sold
Monday	
Tuesday	
Wednesday	
Thursday	
Friday	
= 2 tickets	

Page 16

66. 45 minutes
67. 5/6
68. 439
69. •
•
•
• • • • •
70. feather—1; apple—2; math book—3; TV—4

Bonus Builder #14: 31

Page 17

71. quarter
72.

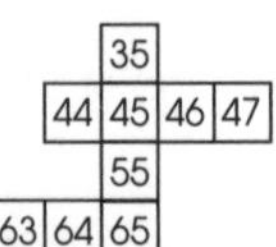

73. triangle—3 sides and 3 angles; diamond—4 sides and 4 angles; pentagon—5 sides and 5 angles; hexagon—6 sides and 6 angles
74. March, June, October
75.

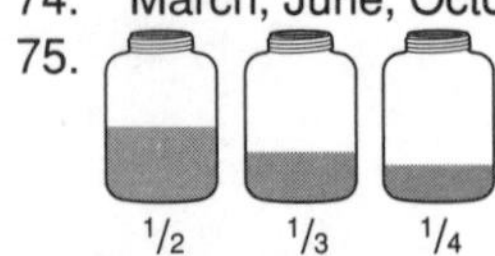

Bonus Builder #15:

1, 2, 4, 7, 11, 16, 22

Pattern Rule: Add 1, add 2, add 3, etc.

Page 18

76. 45, 86, 22, 103
77. 4
78. Answers may vary. Possible answer:
    Weight: pound, gram, ton
    Length: inch, feet, centimeter
79. 5 stickers
80. 4 golf balls

Bonus Builder #16: bagel and milk, bagel and juice, muffin and milk, muffin and juice

Page 19

81. Answers will vary.
82.

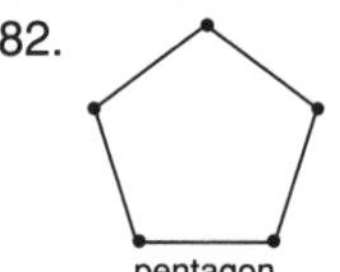

83. 1:00

Bonus Builder #17: 14 days

84. Key: (dotted) = 5/8; (striped) = 3/8

85.

10 less	number	10 more
613	623	633
466	476	486
148	158	168
627	637	647

Page 20

86.

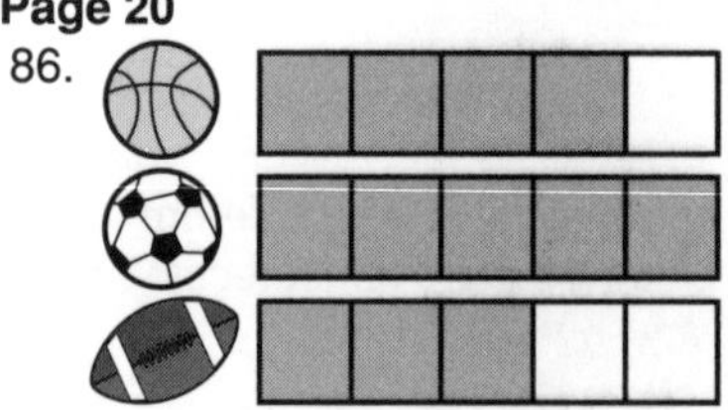

87. Answers will vary. Possible answers: ruler, tape measure, yardstick, meterstick
88. Group 1: addition, plus, sum
    Group 2: subtraction, minus, difference
89. Students should have drawn 2 striped, 4-sided figures.
90. 40 peanuts

Bonus Builder #18:

517—617 826—926 490—590 377—477
319—419 204—304 759—859 637—737

Page 21

91. Congruent figures are figures that have the same size and shape. Students' drawings will vary.
92. 5:30
93. 2 quarters
94. Students should have colored 3 butterflies.
95.

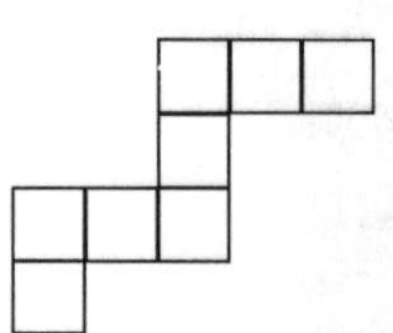

Bonus Builder #19:

527 = 500 + 20 + 7
652 = 600 + 50 + 2
436 = 400 + 30 + 6

Page 22

96. The length of the missing side is 6 cm. The total length of the sides is 20 cm.
97. 2 carrots
98. 2 people
99. The first and third pieces could be used to make a square.

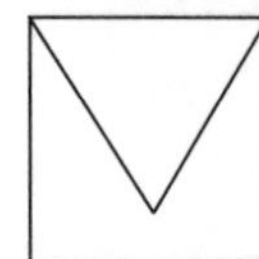

100. fifteen, thirty, one hundred

Bonus Builder #20: greater than

Answer Keys

Page 23

101. $4/6$ or $2/3$; $2/6$ or $1/3$

102. 

103. 8; 25; 24

104. 2 hundreds, 15 tens, and 2 ones = 352
6 hundreds, 3 tens, and 25 ones = 655
4 hundreds and 42 ones = 442
1 hundred, 25 tens, and 7 ones = 357

105.

clover	1	2	3	4	5	6	7	8	9	10
leaves	3	6	9	12	15	18	21	24	27	30

Bonus Builder #21: Answers will vary.

Page 24

106. dogs
107. He has an equal chance of picking an orange and an apple because the same number of each is in the bag.
108. 3 children
109. 238, 288, 384, 484, 586
110. circle

Bonus Builder #22: less than

Page 25

111. 4¢
112. $1/2$; Students' explanations will vary.
113. 477
114. ⚁ ⚀ ⚁ ⚁ ⚀
115. 9 grams

Bonus Builder #23: 20 arms

Page 26

116. 4 bills—$20, $5, $1, $1
117. 3 and 5
118. 483 > 438, 832 > 823, 705 < 750, 4070 < 7040
119. trapezoid and hexagon
120. Answers will vary.

Bonus Builder #24: Answers will vary.

Page 27

121. $1/3$ $1/2$ $1/4$

122. 1,000; 10; 1; 100

123. 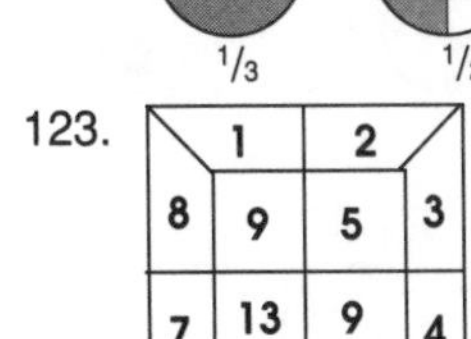

124. 3 triangles
125. Possible explanation: Multiply the number of laps (10) times the number of days (7). 10 x 7 = 70 laps.

Bonus Builder #25:

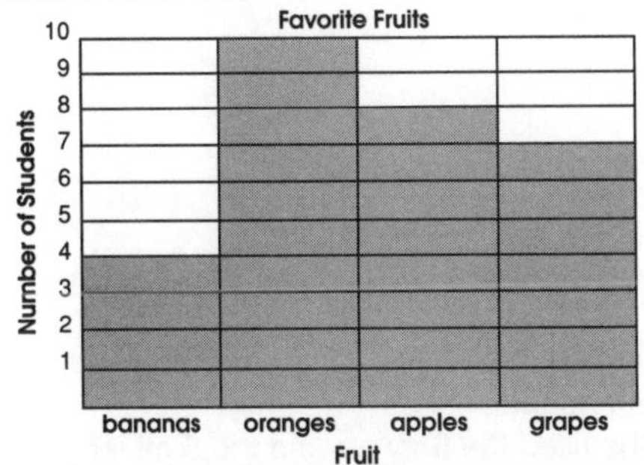

Page 28

126. 172 + 595 = 767; 385 + 194 = 579

127. 

128. 16 square centimeters

129.

60 minutes	1 hour
24 hours	1 day
7 days	1 week

130. $1.20

Bonus Builder #26: $2/4$ c. or $1/2$ c., 1 c.

Page 29

131. 5,432
132. ●■■●■■ or ■●●■●●
133. Students should have drawn a thermometer that reads 50°F. They also should have drawn pictures of themselves dressed appropriately for this temperature in your area.
134. 56
135. 16 and 34

Bonus Builder #27: Answers will vary. However, students' chances of picking a shaded marble and an unshaded marble are equal.

Page 30

136. 10 shoes
137. Figure B is not a polygon because it has a curved side.
138. 2 hours
139. 3 quarters, 2 dimes, 1 nickel

140. 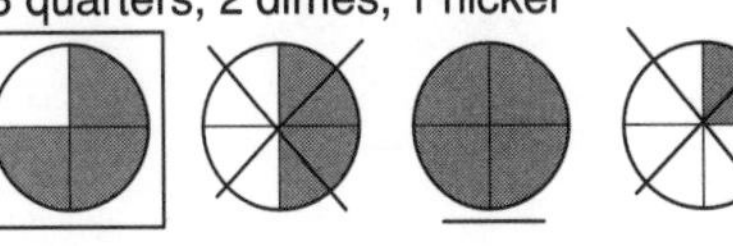

Bonus Builder #28: 25 – 10 = 15
15 – 7 = 8

Page 31

141. 20 tomato plants
142. 13, 21
143. dog—1,4; bird—1,1; cat—3,4; rabbit—4,2
144. No. He arrived at 4:00 P.M., which is later than 3:45 P.M.
145. Drawings will vary. However, the square section of the spinner should be the largest.

Bonus Builder #29: 142

Page 32

146. 5 and 9
147. 869 = 800 + 60 + 9
2,418 = 2,000 + 400 + 10 + 8
305 = 300 + 0 + 5 *or* 300 + 5
148. Possible answers: The figures could be sorted into 2 groups—flat and solid shapes or shapes with curved lines and shapes without curved lines. The figures could be sorted into 3 groups—circular shapes, square shapes, and triangular shapes.
149. 5 packs
150. cheese; $1/3$ is larger than $1/4$.

Bonus Builder #30: 6 possible ways—Dan, Jan, Stan; Dan, Stan, Jan; Jan, Stan, Dan; Jan, Dan, Stan; Stan, Dan, Jan; Stan, Jan, Dan

Page 33

151. neat
152. Thursday, October 11; Saturday, October 13
153. Answers will vary.
154. cup, pint, quart, gallon
155. 2 quarters, 2 dimes, 1 nickel, 2 pennies

Bonus Builder #31: 17 apples; The information given that was not needed to solve the problem was that Jan picked 10 pears.

Answer Keys

Page 34
156. 337
157. The numbers in the pattern increase by 3. The mistake is that the 11 in the pattern should be 12.
158. 238; All of the other numbers have an 8 in the tens place.
159. 18 eggs
160. 20 flowers; 45 flowers
Bonus Builder #32: 25¢

Page 35
161. 23, 47, 91, 100
162. 11 lines
163. Matthew
164. 3 pencils
165. Answers will vary.
Bonus Builder #33: The tree is shorter than 12 feet because it is not twice the height of the 6-foot person standing beside it.

Page 36
166. 34 + 66 = 100   43 + 58 = (101)   56 + 44 = 100
62 + 38 = 100   55 + 50 = (105)
167. No because there are only 12 inches in a foot.
168. 3 quarters
169.

Food Items	Number Ordered
hamburger	○ ○ ○ ○
cheeseburger	○ ○ ○ ○ ○
french fries	○ ○ ○ ◐
onion rings	○ ◐
chicken sandwich	○ ○ ○ ○ ◐
○ = 2 food items	

170. 3 hours
Bonus Builder #34:
John could have pressed the following:
9 [x] [3] [+] [0] [=] 27 or 9 [+] [9] [+] [9] [=] 27
or
9 [x] [2] [+] [9] [=] 27

Page 37
171. Possible answer: Both have 4 sides, both have four angles, and both have straight/parallel lines.
172. 6 oranges, 9 all together
173. $\frac{1}{2}$
174. cotton candy and snow cone
175. Multiply the number of lily pads (4) by the number of frogs (2) on each lily pad.
Bonus Builder #35: The bus will most likely arrive at 7:15 because that is what time it arrived on most days.

Page 38
176. Students should have drawn coins that total 11¢.
177. 3 lollipops
178. 3 hours
179. A. 55   B. 60   C. 100   D. 20
180. 700; 7; 70; 7,000
Bonus Builder #36: $30 + $30 = $60 or $30 x 2 = $60; $70 + $40 = $110

Page 39
181. 9 bikes
182. Katie; 15¢ more
183. 158
184.

dozens	1	2	3	4	5
bagels	12	24	36	48	60

185. 35¢
Bonus Builder #37: 4 marbles; 8 marbles

Page 40
186. No. Possible explanation: Three boxes will hold a total of only 15 books.
187. 6 stars
188. 628 629 630
888 889 890
298 299 300
189. 6 cm
190. 939, 900
Bonus Builder #38: skateboard and kneepads ($30) or helmet and kneepads ($35)

Page 41
191. Possible answer: 1, 3, 4, and 6
192. 5 pieces; 3 pieces
193. inches — yardstick; pint — measuring cup; feet — ruler; pounds — scale

inches	scale
pint	ruler
feet	measuring cup
pounds	yardstick

194.
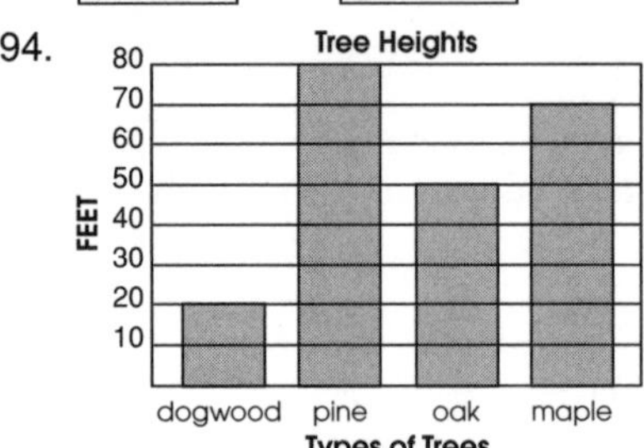

195. 4,375 = 4,000 + 300 + 70 + 5
2,081 = 2,000 + 0 + 80 + 1
6,412 = 6,000 + 400 + 10 + 2
Bonus Builder #39: 2 nickels, 1 quarter, 1 dime, 1 penny

Page 42
196. 10; 100; 1,000; 10,000; 100,000
197. 528, 530, 532, 534, 536
198. Mike—blue, Sara—yellow, Joe—red
199. reading; 15 minutes
200. 1 + 9 + 1 + 1 + 1 + 1 = 14 squares
Bonus Builder #40: 9 gifts

Page 43
201. 19 miles
202. $\frac{1}{3}$ or $\frac{3}{9}$
203.
204. 7 students
205. A and D
Bonus Builder #41:

Number	H	T	O	Sum of digits
423	4	2	3	9
502	5	0	2	7
233	2	3	3	8

Page 44
206. Noah
207. 1994
208. Drawings will vary. Possible drawing:
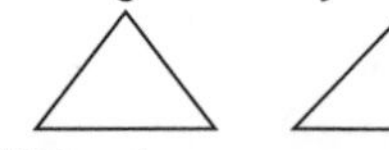
209. 472 books
210. The spinner is not fair because each person's space on the spinner is not equal.
Bonus Builder #42: She filled the 3 ml jar and the 5 ml jar.